Leader's G

student edition

Lee Strobel's THE CASE FOR CHRIST

A journalist's personal investigation of the evidence for Jesus

JANE VOGEL

ZONDERVAN™
GRAND RAPIDS, MICHIGAN 49530 USA

ZONDERVAN™

The Case for Christ— Student Edition Leader's Guide

The Case for Faith—Student Edition Leader's Guide

Requests for information should be addressed to:

Zondervan, *Grand Rapids, Michigan 49530*

ISBN 0-310-25490-6

Interior design by Creative Partners

Printed in the United States of America

04 05 06 07 08 09 10 /❖ DC/ 10 9 8 7 6 5 4 3 2 1

CONTENTS

Read This First!

What you've got This Leader's Guide outlines five sessions to guide youth groups or Sunday school classes through the main points of *The Case for Christ—Student Edition.* (The flip side gives you five more sessions for *The Case for Faith—Student Edition.*) Each session can be accomplished in 45 to 60 minutes. Two scripts are included for short sketches your students can perform for the rest of the church. Use these sketches to highlight what the youth are learning or to promote a study of *The Case for Christ* for adults.

What you need To lead this course effectively, you'll need

- a copy of *The Case for Christ—Student Edition* for each student
- access to a photocopier so you can copy the reproducible student sheets (in the center of the Leader's Guide)
- some basic supplies like pens and Bibles, and some fun supplies like candy and Play-Doh. All the materials required for each session are listed in the "Quick Look" chart at the beginning of each session

What else you should know

- *The Case for Christ—Student Edition* includes some additional material after chapters 2, 4, and 6 that these sessions don't cover. If you find yourself with some extra time during any of the sessions, this bonus material is an ideal length to read aloud and discuss.
- These sessions will work without any outside preparation on your students' part. If you choose to assign reading between sessions, suggested assignments are listed at the end of each session.

SESSION 1

Looking for Answers

Session goals:

In this session, students will

- participate in a bond-building activity
- attempt to provide evidence that Jesus is God, that the Bible can be trusted, and that Jesus rose from the dead
- assess their confidence in God and in their ability to answer tough questions about God
- receive the challenge to investigate the evidence for the case for Christ

Quick Look

Activity	Materials needed	Approximate time
1. Opener: Line Up. Students will work together in small groups to meet challenges, then begin to think about their level of confidence.	• masking tape	5 to 10 minutes
2. Sharing: Confidence Questions. In small groups, students will tell about experiences and explore their confidence in God and in their ability to answer tough questions about God.	• none	15 to 20 minutes
3. Role Plays: Facing the Challenge. Students will be challenged to provide evidence that Jesus is God, that the Bible can be trusted, and that Jesus rose from the dead.	• Bibles	20 to 25 minutes

Quick Look . . . continued

Activity	Materials needed	Approximate time
4. Debriefing: Starting the Investigation. Students will assess their confidence in responding to tough questions about Jesus and receive Lee Strobel's challenge to investigate the evidence for the case for Christ.	• one copy of *The Case for Christ—Student Edition* for each student	5 to 10 minutes

1. Opener: Line Up

Form groups of about eight. (It's okay to have only one group.) Put a strip of masking tape on the floor near each group and instruct the groups to line up, single-file, on their tape lines. Then give instructions like these: **Imagine that the line you are standing on is a construction beam twelve stories up in the air. If you step off the line, you step off the beam. When I give the signal, you must rearrange yourselves without stepping off the beam so that you are lined up alphabetically by first name. Go.**

Watch the groups to make sure they don't step on the floor beside the line. When all the groups are done, give them instructions for a second round: **From this point on, you may not talk. You are still on the beam, still twelve stories up. But now you must line up by birthday, without talking and without stepping off the beam. Go.**

When all the groups are done, debrief with questions like these:

- **What made this activity challenging?**
- **How well did you work together? What did you do to help each other?**
- **What problems did you have working together?**

- **If you had really been up twelve stories, how much confidence would you have had?**

2. Sharing: Confidence Questions

> **FYI**
>
> This activity is more than just a fun way for students to interact. Working together to solve a shared problem can be the first step in building community for a group where not everyone has been together before or strengthening community in a group that has already built relationships.

Have students form groups of three. Give instructions like these: **I will give you a sentence to finish. Take turns talking and listening until everyone in your small group has a chance to finish the sentence. When I say stop, listen for the next sentence to complete. If someone didn't get to finish the sentence before, let that person talk first next time.**

- **When I was eight years old, one of the people I had the most confidence in was . . .**
- **When I was in sixth grade, the ability or quality I felt the most confident about was . . .**
- **The first time I remember thinking about God as someone to put my confidence in was . . .**
- **On a scale of one to ten, I would rate my confidence about explaining what I believe as a . . .**

3. Role Plays: Facing the Challenge

Have students form pairs (it's okay to have one trio). Give each pair a Bible. Tell them to choose one person to be the "asker" in a role play and the other to be the "answerer." Explain that you'll provide the initial question, which the "answerer" should answer. The "asker" can ask follow-up and clarification questions until you call time.

Make sure students understand the instructions, then ask, **I've heard some people say that Jesus is God, but others say that Jesus never claimed to be God at all—people said that about him later. Which is right? If Jesus said he was God, show me or tell me where.**

After thirty seconds or a minute, have partners change roles. Invite the new "answerer" to add to what the first "answerer" already said (if anything).

Continue asking questions and giving each partner a chance to answer, using as many of the following questions or statements as you can:

- **I agree with you that Jesus was a great moral teacher. But why should I believe he was God?**
- **Even if Jesus did say he was God, why should I believe him? He could just be lying.**
- **Suppose Jesus did claim to be God, and suppose he really believed it. Mental hospitals are full of people who think they're Winston Churchill or Gandhi or someone they're not. What's to say that Jesus wasn't crazy?**
- **I know that Christians talk about miracles, but that's unscientific. I've heard that when Jesus seemed to be doing miracles he was actually hypnotizing people to think they'd seen a miracle. Doesn't that seem a lot more likely than a miracle?**
- **I was talking to a Jewish friend about Jesus and prophecies about the Messiah. My friend said Jesus did a bunch of things from the prophecies to fool people into thinking he was the Messiah. Is that true?**
- **Even if Jesus did fulfill Old Testament prophecies, it was probably just a coincidence.**
- **Why do you believe the Bible?**
- **What makes you think the people who wrote the Bible didn't just make it up?**

- **I've heard that at first the stories about Jesus weren't written down. By the time they were, they had grown into legends. That's why the Bible claims Jesus did miracles and rose from the dead.**
- **How can you believe the Bible when it's full of contradictions? For instance, Matthew and Luke both say that Jesus healed a Roman commander's servant. But Matthew says the commander asked Jesus to do it and Luke says the commander sent others to ask. How do you explain that?**
- **I know enough about the Bible to know that the original manuscripts are lost. All we have are copies of copies of copies, and at first all those copies were made by hand. That's how a lot of mistakes got into the Bible.**
- **Why even bother about the Bible? What does it have to do with me?**
- **If Jesus really lived, I would expect that someone besides the Bible authors would have written about him. Did anyone?**
- **Is there any archaeological evidence that the Bible is true? If so, what?**
- **What makes the Bible any more trustworthy than the Book of Mormon?**
- **Is there any evidence *today* that Jesus is real?**
- **Why do you think Jesus came back to life after he died?**
- **I've heard that Jesus didn't really die on the cross. He fainted and looked dead, but after lying in the cool air of the tomb he revived and left. That's why they couldn't find a body there.**
- **I've also heard that the disciples stole Jesus' body. That makes a lot of sense to me. Do you have any reason I shouldn't believe it?**
- **All those stories about people seeing Jesus alive after he died are just legends that grew over time.**
- **If people really did believe they saw Jesus, I bet they were hallucinating.**

- **When people thought they saw Jesus alive after his death, maybe it was just wishful thinking. They wanted so badly to believe it, they convinced themselves that he was alive.**
- **What difference does it make to people today whether or not Jesus came back from the dead 2,000 years ago?**

4. Debriefing: Starting the Investigation

Gather students together and debrief the role-play experience with questions like these:

- **How confident did you feel about responding to the questions and statements in the role plays?**
- **Have you ever been in a similar situation? If so, tell us about it.**
- **Which of the questions do you most wish you had the answers to?**

Hand out copies of *The Case for Christ—Student Edition* and invite students to look them over while you introduce the author, Lee Strobel, by reading aloud the Introduction on pages 7 and 8. Ask students if they can identify with or know anyone like Lee or his friend Ersin. Invite students to accept Lee's challenge to explore the evidence in *The Case for Christ* so they can answer their own questions and those of their friends.

Looking Ahead . . .

If you are assigning reading outside of class, have students read chapters 2, 3, and 4 of *The Case for Christ—Student Edition* before the next session.

PRAYER OPTIONS

If your group already has a particular way they like to pray together, work it into the session wherever it fits best. Otherwise, try one of the following ideas for group prayer:

- **Pass the prayer request:** Recruit two volunteers to write down prayer requests and praises on separate pieces of paper as students share them. Then hand out the papers and go around the circle letting each person pray for the request or praise on his or her paper. This ensures that every request is included, and it makes praying easier for students who might stumble over what to say without the prompt of the paper.
- **Partner prayer:** Have students form pairs and pray for one another. They may choose to share requests stemming from the session (perhaps a question that troubles them, praise for a new insight, or prayer for a friend with whom they want to share Christ) or share more general requests.
- **Prayer for seeking friends:** If your group is made up of Christians, you may wish to focus your prayer for seeking or unbelieving friends. If students can't identify such people in their lives, pray that God will open their eyes to those who need to hear about Christ.

SESSION 2

Who Is This Jesus?

(Chapters 2, 3, and 4 in *The Case for Christ—Student Edition*)

Session goals:

In this session, students will

- explore who Jesus said he was
- address the challenge that Jesus was crazy to claim to be God
- identify ways Jesus fulfilled Old Testament prophecies about the Messiah
- reflect on their own beliefs about who Jesus is

Quick Look

Activity	Materials needed	Approximate time
1. Opener: Three Truths and a Lie: Students will share three facts and a lie about themselves, then win points by correctly guessing which statements are lies.	• pennies or individually wrapped candies	5 to 10 minutes
2. Peer Teaching: Who Is Jesus?: In small groups, students will explore evidence about who Jesus is, then present what they've learned to the other groups.	• one copy of *The Case for Christ—Student Edition* per student • photocopies of student sheets 2-1, 2-2, 2-3 • pens • Bibles • optional: video camera	35 to 40 minutes
3. Application: Convinced?: Students will discuss which evidences they find convincing and what questions they still have.	• none	5 to 10 minutes

1. Opener: Three Truths and a Lie

As students arrive, give each one six pennies or individually wrapped candies. (Make sure they don't eat the candy yet.) When everyone is present, form groups of three or four and give instructions like these: **Tell your small group four things about yourself. Three things should be true; one should be something you just make up. Each person in your small group will try to guess which statement is false. If a person guesses correctly, you must give that person one candy [or penny]. If a person guesses incorrectly, he or she must give you one candy [or penny]. Obviously, you want everybody to guess before you tell anyone whether they are right or wrong! Take turns until everyone has told their four things.**

> **FYI**
>
> Sure, this game has been around a while, but students still love it. It gives them a chance to talk about themselves, to be creative, and to get to know each other a little better. Plus it gives you an easy segue into the theme of today's session.

When the groups are done, let students eat the candy or pocket the pennies.

Make a transition to the focus of today's session by saying something like: **Most people believe Jesus really existed. But a lot of people think the different claims about Jesus are like our four statements—some are true, and some are just made up.**

Explain that this was Lee Strobel's assumption when he started looking into the evidence about Jesus. Read aloud pages 19 and 20 of *The Case for Christ—Student Edition,* stopping after the last full paragraph on page 20. Tell students that in today's session they'll be retracing Lee's investigation into who Jesus is.

2. Peer Teaching: Who Is Jesus?

Form three groups. (Groups can be as small as one person but should be no larger than eight. If you have more than twenty-four students, form more than three groups and assign more than one group to each student sheet.)

Give each group a pen and one copy of either student sheet 2-1, 2-2, or 2-3—a different sheet for each group. Tell students they have about 15 minutes to complete the instructions on their sheet and be ready to teach their material to the other groups. Make sure students have copies of *The Case for Christ—Student Edition,* and set out the supplies listed for this activity. If possible, send groups to different areas to work.

As groups work, circulate to keep them on task and to answer any questions.

After about 20 minutes, bring the groups back together and have them make their presentations. If you have a video camera, tape the presentations for use in session 5.

FYI

The Case for Christ—Student Edition includes some additional material after chapters 2 and 4 that this session doesn't cover. If you find yourself with some extra time during any of the sessions, this bonus material is an ideal length to read aloud and discuss. (If your students are particularly interested in the issue of whether or not Christianity is an intolerant religion (pp. 29-30), you may wish to point them to **The Case for Faith—Student Edition,** which devotes a full chapter to that question.)

3. Application: Convinced?

Help students reflect on their own beliefs about who Jesus is by discussing questions like the following:

- **Which of the evidence presented today do you find most convincing? Why?**
- **Would you say there is a convincing case that Jesus is God? Explain.**
- **What questions do you still have—either questions you wonder about yourself or you know other people wonder about—regarding the evidence that Jesus is God?** (If students raise questions you will address in later sessions, let them know. Otherwise, answer their questions if you can, or make a note of the questions and find the answers before your next session.)

Looking Ahead ...

If you are assigning reading outside of class, have students read chapters 5 and 6 of *The Case for Christ—Student Edition* before the next session.

PRAYER OPTIONS

If your group already has a particular way they like to pray together, work it into the session wherever it fits best. Otherwise, try this idea for group prayer or one of the ideas suggested at the end of session 1.

- **Session-related prayer:** Invite students to choose one of these options to shape their sentence prayers:
  1. Praise Jesus for one of the qualities you discovered about him today. For example, "Jesus, I praise you for being all-knowing. When I'm confused, it's a comfort to know you know everything."
  2. Thank God for one of the things you learned today. For example, "Thank you for giving us the Old Testament prophecies so we can know you really are the promised Messiah."
  3. Ask God to help you with your questions or doubts, using a prayer like the one on page 115 of *The Case for Christ—Student Edition* or one of your own.

SESSION 3

How Reliable Is the Information about Christ?

(Chapters 5 and 6 in *The Case for Christ—Student Edition)*

Session goals:

In this session, students will

- identify difficult objections to trusting Scripture
- explore responses to those objections
- respond personally to Scripture

Quick Look

Activity	Materials needed	Approximate time
1. Opener: Top Tough Objections: Students will identify which questions about the Bible are of most concern to them.	• copies of student sheet 3-1, cut apart and posted around the room • pens	5 to 10 minutes
2. Discussion: Can the Bible Be Trusted?: Students will read and discuss information about their top objections.	• one copy of *The Case for Christ—Student Edition* per student • Bibles	30 to 35 minutes
3. Closing: In God's Word: Students will respond personally to portions of Scripture.	• Psalm 19 option: Bibles • Music option: Scripture-based worship CD; CD player	10 to 15 minutes

1. Opener: Top Tough Objections

Before this session, cut apart copies of student sheet 3-1 and post them around your meeting space.

As students arrive, give each one a pen. Ask them to read all the statements or questions posted around the room, then to put a tally mark on the three they would most like to talk about in this session.

After everyone has marked three choices, tally the votes.

2. Discussion: Can the Bible Be Trusted?

Work through as many objections as you have time for, starting with the one that students have the most interest in. For each objection, use the following format:

- Find the objection in the numbered list below. (The numbers match those on the posted signs.) Read aloud (or invite a volunteer to read aloud) the section from *The Case for Christ—Student Edition* indicated.
- Discuss any additional questions listed under the numbered objections.
- Invite student response with questions like these:
  - **— Does this make sense to you? If not, what part is confusing?**
  - **— Do you find this convincing? Explain.**

1. How do you know whoever wrote the Bible wasn't just making it up?
   (Read "An Informed Audience," pp. 55–57.)
2. I don't deny that a person named Jesus once lived. But the idea that he rose from the dead and all that other stuff is a legend that grew much later.
   (Read "20/30 Hindsight," pp. 57–60.)
3. Because the Bible had to be hand-copied for so many centuries, the Bible we have today is no longer accurate or trustworthy.
   (Read "Playing Telephone," pp. 60–62.)

For fun, play a game of "Telephone." Ask students how that game is both similar and dissimilar to the way the Bible was passed on.

4. How can you believe the Bible when there are so many contradictions in it?

   (Read "Consistency and Contradictions," p. 54; "Contradictory Evidence?" p. 58.)

5. What do I care about the Bible? What does it have to do with me?

   (Read "Words That Work," pp. 62–64.)

Ask students for examples of ways the Bible's guidance has "worked" in their lives. Be ready with an example from your own life. If time permits (or if you need to fill time), ask students to find guidelines from Proverbs or the book of James that have realistic, practical applications for daily living.

6. Did Jesus really live, or is he a fictional character found only in the Bible?

   (Read "Beyond the Biblical Biographies," p. 67.)

7. Can archaeology prove that the Bible is right or wrong?

   (Read pp. 65–66; "Digging for Details," pp. 67–69.)

8. What archaeological evidence is there that the Bible is true?

   (Read "An Archaeologist Looks at Luke," p. 70.)

9. How is the Bible any different from the Book of Mormon?

   (Read "The Book of Mormon," p. 71.)

10. The Bible is so old. Is there any evidence *today* that Christ is real?

    (Read "Contemporary Corroboration," pp. 69–74.)

Invite students to share stories of other lives they know of that have been transformed by the power of the gospel. Ask them to think of people who have influenced them because of the evidence of God's work in their lives. Encourage them to think of small ways in which they see that transformation in their own lives. Challenge them to let their lives be evidence of the truth of the gospel to others.

FYI

The information in this session is great for students who have asked these questions themselves or have been asked (and stumped) by others. But if your students don't feel the need for this information, they may not be very interested in the details. Focus instead on objections 5 and 10, inviting students to focus on experiential corroboration of the truth of the Bible. Spend time in Proverbs and James, as suggested under objection 5, so students can experience the practicality of Scripture for themselves.

3. Closing: In God's Word

Close your session by spending time in God's Word with one of these options:

- Psalm 19 made tangible: Read aloud Psalm 19. Give students 5 minutes to find either something in nature that reveals something about God (vv. 1–6) or a Bible verse that is valuable to them (as described in vv. 7–14). Have each person share his or her choice and why he or she chose it.
- Scripture in song: Play a worship song based on Scripture. (If you're not sure what music is meaningful to your students, ask a few students to bring CDs to your session.) Use the time for quiet reflection, or sing along if your group is into singing.

Looking Ahead ...

If you are assigning reading outside of class, have students read chapters 7, 8, and 9 of *The Case for Christ—Student Edition* before the next session.

PRAYER OPTIONS

If your group already has a particular way they like to pray together, work it into the session wherever it fits best. Otherwise, try one of the ideas suggested at the end of session 1.

SESSION 4

Can a Dead Man Come Back to Life?

(Chapters 7, 8, and 9 in *The Case for Christ – Student Edition)*

Session goals:

In this session, students will

- evaluate the theory that Jesus didn't really die on the cross
- explore evidence for and against the theory that someone moved Jesus' body
- evaluate theories attempting to disprove the post-resurrection sightings of Jesus
- reflect on their own assurance about life after death

Quick Look

Activity	Materials needed	Approximate time
1. Opener: "Easter Egg" Hunt. Students will hunt for hidden candy and share favorite Easter memories or traditions.	• candy	5 to 10 minutes
2. Listening: Did Jesus Fake His Death? Students will hear the details of crucifixion.	• optional: wooden cross, nails, hammer	about 10 minutes
3. Projects: What Happened to the Body? Students will work in teams to explore evidence for and against the theory that someone moved Jesus' body.	• student sheets 4-1 and 4-2 • Play-Doh® • string • scissors	20 to 25 minutes

Quick Look . . . continued

Activity	Materials needed	Approximate time
4. Skimming: What Did Jesus Do after Easter? Students will evaluate theories attempting to disprove the post-resurrection sightings of Jesus.	• *The Case for Christ—Student Edition*	5 to 10 minutes
5. Reflection: The Resurrection of Debbie: Students will listen to a personal testimony of faith, reflect on their own assurance about life after death, and pray.	• *The Case for Christ—Student Edition*	about 5 minutes

1. Opener: "Easter Egg" Hunt

Before the session, hide pieces of candy around your meeting space.

When everyone has arrived, form two teams. Explain that you've arranged an Easter egg hunt for them in your room (except that you probably won't have Easter eggs, so tell them what the candy is). This hunt is a contest; in order for a team to win, each person on the team must pick up a piece of candy from its hiding place (not from another person). That means if one team member has already found a piece of candy, he or she would be wise to help another team member find a piece. The first team in which all members have a piece of candy wins.

Give the signal for teams to begin.

When a team has won, congratulate them, but let the other team continue until everyone has a piece of candy. (If it's quiet candy, let them eat it now; if it's noisy, save it till activity 3 so students aren't distracted during activity 2.)

When everyone is seated, ask kids to share favorite Easter traditions or memories. Explain that today's session focuses on a question that is a stumbling block to many people investigating Christianity: Did Jesus really come back from the dead on that first Easter?

2. Listening: Did Jesus Fake His Death?

Introduce this section by reading aloud the second and third paragraphs on page 82 of *The Case for Christ—Student Edition,* which raises the question of whether or not Jesus could have faked his death and subsequent resurrection. Tell your students you'll give them some information and let them draw their own conclusions. Ask them to listen quietly and without distracting others.

The passage on Christ's crucifixion in *The Case for Christ—Student Edition* is very powerful. Rather than trying to paraphrase it, simply read it aloud and let students absorb its impact. Start reading at the heading "Sweating Blood" on page 84 and read through the end of the chapter on page 88, pausing after "You can draw your own conclusions" in the third paragraph on page 88 for students to reflect and respond aloud if they wish.

FYI

You can add visual and auditory potency to this experience by bringing a large wooden cross into your meeting space. When you read the description of the nails piercing Christ's wrists (p. 86), have a student you've enlisted in advance pound two large nails into the cross.

3. Projects: What Happened to the Body?

Explain that one theory for why Jesus' grave was empty on Easter is that someone took the body. Tell students you need two teams to explore some of the evidence for and against that theory. Invite students to choose whether they would like to be on a drama team or an art team. (If your group is so large that team size is unmanageable, make several teams and give them all the same assignment.)

Give the drama team a copy of student sheet 4-1 and make sure each student has a copy of *The Case for Christ—Student Edition.* If possible, let the team go to a separate space to work.

Give the art team a copy of student sheet 4-2, Play-Doh, string, and scissors. Provide a surface for them to put the Play-Doh on if you don't have an appropriate surface in your meeting space. Tell both teams they have about 15 minutes.

After the 15 minutes are up, have the teams present their projects. Debrief with questions like:

- **Based on what you learned, how convincing do you find the theory that the disciples stole the body? Explain.**
- **What other possibilities could account for Jesus' body being gone from the tomb?** If students suggest any of the other theories addressed in chapter 8, point them to the relevant section and discuss it.

4. Skimming: What Did Jesus Do after Easter?

Introduce the issue of the post-resurrection sightings by reading pages 100 and 101 aloud from *The Case for Christ—Student Edition,* up to the heading "500 Eyewitnesses." Read aloud the question in the "Your Call" box on page 102 and discuss it with your students.

Have students turn with you to page 103 and follow along as you highlight the three possibilities on pages 103–106. Ask volunteers to read the bulleted lists in each section. Ask: **Do you agree with Lee that legends, hallucinations, and wishful thinking are not convincing explanations for the accounts of all the people who saw Jesus after his death? Why or why not?**

5. Reflection: The Resurrection of Debbie

Tell students you'd like to share with them a more personal perspective on the resurrection, and you'd like them to think about their own response to it. Invite them to follow along or just listen as you read "The Resurrection of Debbie" aloud from the box on page 109 in *The Case for Christ—Student Edition.*

When you're done reading, quietly ask students to close their eyes and reflect on whether or not they share Gary Habermas's assurance in life after death. Invite them to talk silently with God about it.

Looking Ahead ...

If you are assigning reading outside of class, have students read the Conclusion of *The Case for Christ—Student Edition* before the next session.

PRAYER OPTIONS

If your group already has a particular way they like to pray together, work it into the session wherever it fits best. Otherwise, try one of the ideas suggested at the end of session 1.

SESSION 5

Ready!

(Chapters 7, 8, and 9 in *The Case for Christ—Student Edition)*

Session goals:

In this session, students will

- review what they've learned about Jesus, the Bible, and the resurrection
- provide evidence that Jesus is God, that the Bible can be trusted, and that Jesus rose from the dead
- reflect on the next step they need to take as a result of this course

Quick Look

Activity	Materials needed	Approximate time
1. Opener: Line Up: Students will work together in small groups to meet challenges, then compare their readiness level to the first time they did this exercise at the beginning of the course.	• masking tape	5 to 10 minutes
2. Review: Tough Questions: In small groups, students will review what they've learned about Jesus, the Bible, and the resurrection.	• copies of student sheets 5-1, 5-2, and 5-3 • pens • one copy of *The Case for Christ—Student Edition* for each student • optional: video of presentations from session 2	15 to 20 minutes

Quick Look . . . continued

Activity	Materials needed	Approximate time
3. Role Plays: Facing the Challenge: Students will be challenged to provide evidence that Jesus is God, that the Bible can be trusted, and that Jesus rose from the dead.	• Bibles • completed student sheets from activity	20 to 25 minutes
4. Application: Where Do We Go from Here?: Students will reflect on the next step they need to take as a result of this course.	• *The Case for Christ—Student Edition*	5 to 10 minutes

1. Opener: Line Up

Begin the final session of this course the same way you began the first session.

Form groups of about eight. (It's okay to have only one group.) Put a strip of masking tape on the floor near each group and instruct the groups to line up, single-file, on their tape lines. Then give instructions like these: **Imagine that the line you are standing on is a construction beam twelve stories up in the air. If you step off the line, you step off the beam. When I give the signal, you must rearrange yourselves without stepping off the beam so that you are lined up alphabetically by first name. Go.**

Watch the groups to make sure they don't step on the floor beside the line. When all the groups are done, give them instructions for a second round: **From this point on, you may not talk. You are still on the beam, still twelve stories up. But now you must line up by birthday, without talking and without stepping off the beam. Go.**

When all the groups are done, debrief with questions like these:

- **Was this activity easier this time than when you did it at the beginning of this course? Explain.**
- **What other situations can you think of that are easier when you know what is expected of you or when you are prepared with some experience?**

2. Review: Tough Questions

Tell students that today they'll have a chance to test themselves—to see if they are any better prepared to respond to tough questions about Jesus, the Bible, and the resurrection. Tell them they'll have one more chance to get ready.

Form three teams: Response Teams 1, 2, and 3. Give each member of Response Team 1 a pen and a copy of student sheet 5-1, each member of Response Team 2 a pen and a copy of student sheet 5-2, and each member of Response Team 3 a pen and a copy of student sheet 5-3. Read aloud the directions (which are the same on each sheet), then give the teams about 20 minutes to review as a team. (Make sure students have their copies of *The Case for Christ—Student Edition.*)

> **FYI**
>
> If you videotaped the presentations in session 2, you can play that tape now as a part of the review.

3. Role Play: Facing the Challenge

After about 20 minutes, gather the Response Teams together. Direct questions to each team from their student sheet, taking questions for each of the three sheets in order so that two teams don't sit idle while one answers all the questions. Encourage Response Teams to designate a different team member to answer each question, but allow them to confer if the team member is unsure how to answer.

Note that the first question for Response Team 2 and Response Team 3 requires thought and synthesis of all the material they have reviewed. Don't hold out for one "correct" answer; listen to hear how well students can summarize as they answer.

The final question for Response Team 2 and Response Team 3 calls for a personal response. It's okay if Response Teams share the examples from the book, but encourage them also to think of their own examples.

4. Application: Where Do We Go from Here?

When you have finished with the student sheets, have students form pairs. Ask them to share their responses to the following questions with their partners:

- **On a scale of 1 to 10, how confident are you about explaining what you believe?**
- **How does that confidence level compare with your confidence level at the end of the first session of this course?**
- **If you haven't grown in confidence, why do you think that is? If you have grown in confidence, how might you use that increased confidence?**
- **What is the next step you should take? Do you need to act on what you've discovered about Jesus and make or renew a commitment to him? Or are you already firm in your own commitment, but you need to talk with someone you know is asking these questions?**

Don't miss the opportunity to invite students to make a commitment to Christ. You can offer that invitation in your own words, or you can read or paraphrase Lee's invitation on pages 114 and 115 in *The Case for Christ—Student Edition.*

Close your time together with prayers of commitment to taking the next step.

Did Jesus Really Think He Was God?

Your task is to prepare a presentation to teach the other groups who Jesus thought he was. You'll find the information you need on pages 21–28 in *The Case for Christ—Student Edition.* You may also use Bibles to look up the passages given in the book.

Your presentation must include every member of your small group and must last no more than 5 minutes total.

Who did Jesus say he was?

Choose one of the following ways to dramatize this material for the other groups, or come up with an idea of your own:

- Act out a series of scenes illustrating the events and what each person said.
- Produce a news segment reporting on the various events.
- Interview each of the characters on late-night television. (But remember to make sure that what the people said in the Bible comes through clearly and accurately.)

Be sure to include the following information in this part of your presentation.

- Peter's statement (see p. 23):
- Jesus' response:
- Jesus' statement about himself (see p. 23 and John 10:24–33):
- The crowd's response:
- Thomas's statement (see p. 25):
- Jesus' response:
- Based on the above, do you think Jesus was claiming to be God?
- Why didn't Jesus come right out and say, "I'm God!" instead of "I and the Father are One?" (See p. 24.)

Was Jesus lying?

Read the section on pages 25–28 and summarize your findings here.

Now decide how to communicate this to the other groups. Here are some ideas, or you can come up with your own:

- If you do an interview or newscast format for the first part of your presentation, you can include this information as a "man-on-the-street" interview or an editorial segment.
- Stage a brief debate on the pros and cons of lying about being God. Ask your audience to decide whether or not they think Jesus would be willing to die for a lie.

Was Jesus Crazy to Claim to Be God?

Your task is to prepare a presentation to teach the other groups who Jesus thought he was. You'll find the information you need on pages 31–38 in *The Case for Christ—Student Edition.* You may also use Bibles to look up the passages given in the book.

Your presentation must include every member of your small group and must last no more than 5 minutes total.

Was Jesus crazy?

Decide how to communicate the material in the box on page 33 to the other groups. Consider these ideas or come up with one of your own:

- List the symptoms in the left column one at a time. After each one, ask someone from the other groups to read the passage(s) listed in the corresponding right column and draw their own conclusions.
- Act out a scene between psychologists in a staff meeting on Jesus' mental health, going through the checklist in the table.

Miracle-worker or master hypnotist?

Read pages 34 (starting after the space) through the top of 37. Be ready to explain what miracles have to do with the charge that Jesus was crazy, and decide how to communicate the information in the chart on page 36–37. Adapt the suggestions above, or come up with your own.

Did Jesus Match the Identity of the Messiah?

Your task is to prepare a presentation to teach the other groups who Jesus thought he was. You'll find the information you need on pages 39–48 in *The Case for Christ—Student Edition*. You may also use Bibles to look up the passages given in the book.

Complete this sheet as you plan your presentation; you'll use the information again in a later session.

Your presentation must include every member of your small group and must last no more than 5 minutes total.

Messianic maneuvering?

Read the sections "Probing the Prophecies" and "Messianic Maneuvering" on pages 44–45 of *The Case for Christ—Student Edition*. Then decide how to communicate that material and the material in the box on page 46. Consider these ideas or come up with one of your own:

- Present the information in "readers' theater" style, with one person reading all the prophecies and another reading all the fulfillments.
- Act out a scene between a Jewish person describing his or her understanding of the Messiah by reading the prophecies from the box and a Christian describing his or her understanding of Christ (which means "Messiah") by describing how Jesus fulfilled each.

Coincidence?

Read the section "Coincidence" on pages 45 and 47. How can you help the other groups picture these odds? Here are some ideas. Maybe you have some others.

- Write on a piece of paper or a whiteboard "Odds: 1 in 170" and ask who thinks it could be coincidence if Jesus fulfilled prophecies when the odds of doing so are 1 in 170. Then add a zero and ask who still thinks so. Keep going until you've put up all 17 zeroes. Explain Dr. Stoner's calculations.
- Tear up a whole bunch of little pieces of paper. Mark just one with an X. Put them all on the table or floor with the X facing down. Choose a volunteer to try to pick the one with the X. See how many tries it takes. Then explain the odds described in the tile example on page 47.

Top Tough Objections

1. How do you know whoever wrote the Bible wasn't just making it up?
   (An "Informed Audience," pp. 55–57)

2. I don't deny that a person named Jesus once lived. But the idea that he rose from the dead and all that other stuff is a legend that grew up much later.
   ("20/30 Hindsight," pp. 57–60)

3. Because the Bible had to be hand-copied for so many centuries, the Bible we have today is no longer accurate or trustworthy.
   ("Playing Telephone," pp. 60–62)

4. How can you believe the Bible when there are so many contradictions in it?
   ("Consistency and Contradictions," p. 54; "Contradictory Evidence?" p. 58)

5. What do I care about the Bible? What does it have to do with me?
   ("Words That Work," pp. 62–64)

6. Did Jesus really live, or is he a fictional character found only in the Bible?
   ("Beyond the Biblical Biographies," p. 67)

7. Can archaeology prove that the Bible is right or wrong?
   (pp. 65–66; "Digging for Details," p. 67–69)

8. What archaeological evidence is there that the Bible is true?
   ("An Archaeologist Looks at Luke," p. 70)

9. How is the Bible any different from the Book of Mormon?
   ("The Book of Mormon," p. 71)

10. The Bible is so old. Is there any evidence today that Christ is real?
    ("Contemporary Corroboration," pp. 69–74)

Drama Team: What Happened to the Body?

Read pages 92–96 of *The Case for Christ—Student Edition* (you can skip the shaded boxes on pages 92 and 93).

Prepare a skit or role play showing what would have had to happen in order for the disciples to steal Jesus' body from his grave. Follow these guidelines:

- Include as much information from pages 92–96 as you can, in whatever creative ways you can.
- Every member of your team must be involved. Team members can play inanimate objects, people, or whatever.
- You must be ready to present your skit in 15 minutes.

Art Team: What Happened to the Body?

Read pages 92–96 of *The Case for Christ—Student Edition* (you can skip the shaded boxes on pages 92 and 93).

Using the supplies provided, create a model of Jesus' grave based on the information on pages 92–96. Make sure that everyone is involved in the process in some way.

Be ready to show and explain your model in 15 minutes.

Response Team 1: Who Is This Jesus?

Make sure every member of your Response Team can respond confidently to the following questions and challenges. If you don't know a good response, look up the relevant pages in *The Case for Christ—Student Edition* (listed in parentheses).

- I've heard some people say that Jesus is God, but others say that Jesus never claimed to be God at all—people said that about him later. Which is right? If Jesus said he was God, show me or tell me where. (pp. 23–25)
- I agree with you that Jesus was a great moral teacher. But why should I believe he was God? (p. 26)
- Even if Jesus did say he was God, why should I believe him? He could just be lying. (pp. 25–28)
- Suppose Jesus did claim to be God, and suppose he really believed it. Mental hospitals are full of people who think they're Winston Churchill or Gandhi or someone they're not. What's to say that Jesus wasn't crazy? (pp. 32–34)
- I know that Christians talk about miracles, but that's unscientific. I've heard that when Jesus seemed to be doing miracles he was actually hypnotizing people to think they'd seen a miracle. Doesn't that seem a lot more likely than a miracle? (pp. 35–37)
- I was talking to a Jewish friend about Jesus and prophecies about the Messiah. My friend said Jesus did a bunch of things from the prophecies to fool people into thinking he was the Messiah. Is that true? (p. 45)
- Even if Jesus did fulfill Old Testament prophecies, it was probably just a coincidence. (pp. 45–47)

Response Team 2: How Reliable Is the Information about Christ?

Make sure every member of your Response Team can respond confidently to the following questions and challenges. If you don't know a good response, look up the relevant pages in *The Case for Christ—Student Edition* (listed in parentheses).

- Why do you believe the Bible?
- What makes you think the people who wrote the Bible didn't just make it up? (pp. 55–57)
- I've heard that at first the stories about Jesus weren't written down. By the time they were, they had grown into legends. That's why the Bible claims Jesus did miracles and rose from the dead. (pp. 57, 59–60)
- How can you believe the Bible when it's full of contradictions? For instance, Matthew and Luke both say that Jesus healed a Roman commander's servant. But Matthew says the commander asked Jesus to do it and Luke says the commander sent others to ask. How do you explain that? (pp. 54, 58)
- I know enough about the Bible to know that the original manuscripts are lost. All we have are copies of copies of copies. And at first all those copies were made by hand. That's how a lot of mistakes got into the Bible. (pp. 60–62)
- Why even bother about the Bible? What does it have to do with me? (pp. 62–64)
- If Jesus really lived, I would expect that someone besides the Bible authors would have written about him. Did anyone? (p. 67)
- Is there any archaeological evidence that the Bible is true? If so, what? (pp. 67–70)
- What makes the Bible any more trustworthy than the Book of Mormon? (p. 71)
- Is there any evidence *today* that Jesus is real? (pp. 69–74)

Response Team 3: Who Is This Jesus?

Make sure every member of your Response Team can respond confidently to the following questions and challenges. If you don't know a good response, look up the relevant pages in *The Case for Christ—Student Edition* (listed in parentheses).

- Why do you think Jesus came back to life after he died?
- I've heard that Jesus didn't really die on the cross. He fainted and looked dead, but after lying in the cool air of the tomb he revived and left. That's why they couldn't find a body there. (pp. 83–88)
- I've also heard that the disciples stole Jesus' body. That makes a lot of sense to me. Do you have any reason I shouldn't believe it? (pp. 92–96)
- All those stories about people seeing Jesus alive after he died are just legends that grew over time. (pp. 103–104)
- If people really did believe they saw Jesus, I bet they were hallucinating. (pp. 104–105)
- Or maybe when people thought they saw Jesus alive after his death, it was just wishful thinking. They wanted so badly to believe it, they did. (pp. 105–106)
- What difference does it make to people today anyway, whether or not Jesus came back from the dead 2,000 years ago? (p. 107)

Two Short Scripts

The Case for Christ—Student Edition

How to use these scripts. These scripts allow your students to present two short sketches depicting "before" and "after" scenes. Script 1, the "before" scene, highlights the need for convincing evidence for the case for Christ. Script 2, "after," shows how being equipped with evidence can give believers confidence in sharing their faith and give seekers the evidence they need to make a decision for Christ.

Consider these options for using the sketches:

- Present Script 1 to your youth group to promote the study of *The Case for Christ—Student Edition*. Use Script 2 to celebrate what they've learned at the end of the course.
- Present the sketches to the whole church to highlight what the youth group is doing. You can present Script 1 at the beginning of your course, then Script 2 at the conclusion, or you can present them back-to-back at the end of the course.
- Use the sketches to promote a study for adults of *The Case for Christ.*

Staging the sketches. Use your students as actors. There's a part for you, too! Photocopy the scripts so every player has one. Nonspeaking parts are flexible in number so that you can involve all your students. Keep sets and props simple; let the audience rely on their imaginations. Tips for sets and staging are included in the scripts.

You can adapt the sketches to your own setting by using your students' real names, replacing the activities mentioned with things your students do together, and so on. Have fun!

Script 1: Before

Cast:

Chris (Christian student)

Friends (as few or as many students as you have; assign the "friends" lines any way you wish)

Youth leader

Setting: A bowling alley. Set up chairs facing the audience. As students talk, they can be changing their shoes, getting soft drinks (use empty cups) from a counter (any flat surface will work), looking at the bowling scores (a plain sheet of paper). The action isn't important; just give people a little action so they have something to do with their hands. If you want to get fancy, set up a disco light to simulate "cosmic" or "laser" bowling.

Friend 1:	Look at that! I got three strikes in a row in the last game!
Friend 2:	Yeah, but only because they put the bumpers in!
Friend 3:	Hey, let's come again tomorrow for laser bowling, only we can all wear white shirts. I love the way they glow in the black lights.
Friends:	Okay. Sounds good. Count me in.
Friend 3:	What about you, Chris? Wanna bowl again tomorrow night?
Chris:	Nah. I've got youth group tomorrow night.
Any Friend:	Youth group? You mean at church?
Chris:	Yeah. You want to come? It's pretty awesome. We play some great games, do some Bible study, hang out with cool people—stuff like that.
Any Friend:	Bible study? Why do you waste your time on that? You don't really believe that stuff, do you?

Chris:	Yeah, I do.
Any Friend:	Why?
Chris:	Uh . . . because . . . uh . . . it's God's message to us.
Any Friend:	What makes you think the people who wrote it didn't just make it up? I've always heard those stories are just legends.
Chris:	[Friends pepper Chris with questions, and Chris turns from one to another, stammering but not able to answer questions.]
Any Friend:	Besides, the Bible is full of contradictions. How can you believe something that contradicts itself?
Any Friend:	Yeah. What makes the Bible any different from any other religious book? Like the Book of Mormon—how is the Bible any different from that?
Any Friend:	And anyway, the Bible's so old. What does it have to do with you?
Chris:	Well, it tells me about Jesus. You know—about he's God.
Any Friend:	I don't think Jesus ever meant people to think he was God. I mean, he was a great moral teacher, but I don't think he ever claimed to be any more than that.
Any Friend:	Even if he did, that wouldn't prove anything. Mental hospitals are full of people who think they're Winston Churchill or Gandhi or someone they're not. What's to say that Jesus wasn't crazy?
Any Friend:	Or lying.
Chris:	Well, a crazy man or a liar couldn't come back from the dead, could he?
Any Friend:	Pull-eeze. Nobody could come back from the dead. That's just a bunch of wishful thinking.

Any Friend: I've heard that Jesus didn't really die on the cross. He just faked it, or fainted, or something. That's why people said he was alive later.

Any Friend: Well, I heard that the disciples stole Jesus' body. That makes a lot of sense to me. Do you have any reason I shouldn't believe it?

Any Friend: I don't know why we're even talking about this. What difference does it make to people today anyway, whether Jesus came back from the dead 2000 years ago?

[Friends leave. One turns back and talks to Chris]

Remaining Friend: You've got to admit, those are pretty good questions. I'm kind of interested in this Jesus of yours, but I need some evidence. Is there any evidence *today* that Jesus is real?

[Chris opens mouth, but doesn't have anything to say. After a moment, remaining friend shrugs and walks away.]

Youth leader wraps up with an explanation of what the youth will be studying, or a challenge to adults, or whatever you've decided your purpose is for this sketch.

Script 2: After

Cast:

Chris (Christian student)

Friends (as few or as many students as you have; assign the "friends" lines any way you wish)

Setting: The same bowling alley as in Script 1. Friends are pulling on shoes as Chris enters.

Friend 1: Hey, Chris! Glad you could make it!

Friend 2: Yeah—crazy bowling isn't the same without your patented double-skip, 180-spin, through-the-legs backward roll! [demonstrates]

Friend 3: Skipping youth group tonight?

Chris: No, youth group was last night.

Any Friend: There's no hard feelings just because we don't buy into all that stuff about the Bible and Jesus, is there?

Chris: No. Actually, I'm kind of glad you asked all those questions last time. It made me think a lot about what I believe and why.

Any Friend: Whatever. I still can't believe any intelligent person would believe in God. No offense.

Chris: You might change your mind if you really looked at all the evidence. I've got answers to your questions now if you're interested.

Any Friend: Yeah, maybe we could talk about it after we bowl a few games.

[Other Friends shrug or make noncommittal responses—"Maybe." "Okay." "We'll see."]

Any Friend: Hey, our lane's open. [Points offstage as if to lane.] Go get a ball, Chris.

[All Friends but one exit to one side as if going to their lane. Remaining Friend from end of Script 1 walks with Chris as if to pick out a ball.]

Remaining Friend: What kind of evidence do you mean?

Chris: Well, let me tell you what I found out about how you can trust what the Bible says about Jesus. [They exit, with Chris trailing off the beginning of an explanation.] You see, I found out that non-Christian historians actually wrote about Jesus, too, and what they wrote agrees with what the Bible tells us . . .

Leader's Guide

student edition

Lee Strobel's The Case for Faith

A journalist investigates the toughest objections to Christianity

JANE VOGEL

ZONDERVAN™
GRAND RAPIDS, MICHIGAN 49530 USA

CONTENTS

Read This First!

What you've got This Leader's Guide outlines five sessions to guide youth groups or Sunday school classes through the main points of *The Case for Faith—Student Edition.* (The flip side gives you five more sessions for *The Case for Christ—Student Edition.*) Each session can be accomplished in 45 to 60 minutes. Two scripts are included for short sketches your students can perform for the rest of the church. Use these sketches to highlight what the youth are learning or to promote a study of *The Case for Faith* for adults.

What you need To lead this course effectively, you'll need

- a copy of *The Case for Faith—Student Edition* for each student
- access to a photocopier so you can copy the reproducible student sheets (in the center of the Leader's Guide)
- some basic supplies like pens and Bibles, and some fun supplies like ping-pong balls and Scrabble tiles. All the materials required for each session are listed in the "Quick Look" chart at the beginning of each session.

What else you should know These sessions will work without any outside preparation on your students' part. If you choose to assign reading between sessions, suggested assignments are listed at the end of each session.

SESSION 1

How Can a Good God Allow Suffering?

(Objection #1 in *The Case for Faith—Student Edition*)

Session goals:

In this session, students will

- identify obstacles to faith in Jesus;
- explore responses to the objection that a good God would not allow suffering;
- reflect on how God has worked through painful situations in their own lives.

Quick Look

Activity	Materials needed	Approximate time
1. Opener: Obstacle Course: Students will run an obstacle course, then compare the experience to real-life obstacles to faith.	• outdoor option: anything you can use as obstacles: traffic cones, Hula Hoops, etc. • table-top option: ping-pong balls, ordinary objects for obstacles (cups, books, etc.)	10 to 15 minutes
2. Scripture Search: Why Does God Allow Suffering?: In small groups, students will read passages from Scripture and *The Case for Faith—Student Edition,* then share their findings.	• a copy of *The Case for Faith—Student Edition* for each student • pens • Bibles • student sheets 1-1 through 1-6	25 to 30 minutes
3. Story-Sharing: Making It Personal: Students will tell about their own experiences with hard times and how they have seen God work through those experiences.	• optional: invite someone who has gone through a painful experience to talk with your students	10 to 15 minutes

1. Opener: Obstacle Course

Introduce the idea of obstacles to faith by having students run an obstacle course. Use or adapt one of the following options to fit your time, climate, and space restrictions.

- Outdoor obstacle course: Set up a course outdoors for your students to run. Easy-to-set-up obstacles include running up and down steps, around garbage cans, under or over railings. With a few more supplies, you can set up cones to run around, a limbo bar to go under, Hula Hoops to twirl or to step in, etc. If you have a playground near your meeting space, use the monkey bars, swings, beams, etc.
- Indoor obstacle course: If you have a big indoor space, you can adapt the outdoor course ideas to use indoors.
- Table-top obstacle course: This option works if you don't have time or space to do a larger course, or if your students are wearing clothes inappropriate for that kind of physical activity. Enlist students to set up a mini-course on the floor or a table-top, using whatever objects you can easily provide: cups, pens, books, etc. Then have students "run" the course by trying to blow ping-pong balls through the course. Time them to see which team or student wins.

FYI

You can turn this activity into a team-building event by requiring team members to run the course together, with each member in physical contact with the person in front and behind. For instance, they can run with hands on the shoulders of the person in front, do monkey bars with legs wrapped around the waist of the person in front, and so on.

Whatever course options you use, have students compete in teams so that you don't end up with an individual, last-place "loser."

Debrief this activity with questions like these:

- **How is real life sometimes like running an obstacle course?**
- **What are some of the obstacles people your age face?**
- **What obstacles do you think keep people from having faith in Jesus?**
- **What are the obstacles that sometimes challenge you in your faith?**

Explain that this course will explore some of the most troublesome obstacles to Christian faith.

2. Scripture Search: Why Does God Allow Suffering?

Form six groups. (A group can be as small as one person. If you have fewer than six students, give each group more than one student sheet.)

Hand out Bibles, *The Case for Faith—Student Edition,* pens, and Student Sheets 1-1 through 1-6—a different one to each group. Give groups about 10 minutes to complete their sheets.

After about 10 minutes, call the groups back together and have them report their findings to the other groups.

FYI

Students know intuitively that these "answers" to the problem of suffering aren't necessarily satisfying or comforting when you're in the middle of the pain. Acknowledge that often we don't see God working until after the fact, and encourage students to comfort struggling friends first of all with their presence, rather than with a list of answers.

3. Story-Sharing: Making It Personal

Invite students to share how they've seen God use a tough situation in their lives to train or prepare them in some way, to redirect them when

they needed to make a midcourse correction, to bring something positive out of the situation, or to get their attention and bring them closer to him. If you have students who are not believers, invite them to share stories of seeing something good come out of suffering, then challenge them to consider whether God might have worked in that situation.

FYI

If someone in your church or someone else you know has gone through a significant struggle and is willing to talk with your students about it, invite that person to share those experiences as a guest at this point in the session.

It isn't always easy for students to think of an example off the tops of their heads, so be ready to set an example by sharing your own experience first. You can also read aloud the section "The God Who Holds Our Hands" on pages 25–27 of *The Case for Faith—Student Edition.*

Looking Ahead ...

If you are assigning reading outside of class, have students read Objections #2 and #3 in *The Case for Faith—Student Edition* before the next session.

PRAYER OPTIONS

If your group already has a particular way they like to pray together, work it into the session wherever it fits best. Otherwise, try one of the following ideas for group prayer:

- **Session-related prayer:** Invite students to choose one of these options to shape their sentence prayers:
  - Thank God for a specific way he has worked through a painful situation in your life.
  - Ask for help dealing with an unresolved difficulty.
  - Ask God to help a friend dealing with a painful situation.
- **Pass the prayer request:** Recruit two volunteers to write down prayer requests and praises on separate pieces of paper as students share them. Then hand out the papers and go around the circle letting each person pray for the request or praise on his or her paper. This ensures that every request is included, and it makes praying easier for students who might stumble over what to say without the prompt of the paper.
- **Partner prayer:** Have students form pairs and pray for one another. They may choose to share requests stemming from the session (perhaps a painful situation they face, an obstacle to faith that troubles them, praise for a new insight, or prayer for a friend with whom they want to share Christ) or share more general requests.
- **Prayer for seeking friends:** If your group is made up of Christians, you may wish to focus your prayer for seeking or unbelieving friends who face obstacles to faith. If students can't identify such people in their lives, pray that God will open their eyes to those who need to hear about Christ.

SESSION 2

With Science and Evolution, Who Needs God?

(Objections #2 and #3 in *The Case for Faith—Student Edition*)

Session goals:

In this session, students will

- observe an object lesson demonstrating the relationship of miracles to science
- explore five reasons to believe God exists
- research data about the theory of evolution and the theory of intelligent design
- reflect on their own beliefs regarding science and God

Quick Look

Activity	Materials needed	Approximate time
1. Object Lesson: The Falling Apple: Students will use the scientific method to predict how the law of gravity will work, then observe an intervention that changes the expected outcome.	• apple • other small objects to drop, such as a pen, book, coin, keys, shoe	5 to 10 minutes
2. Skimming: Top Five Reasons to Give God the Benefit of the Doubt: Students will skim material in *The Case for Faith—Student Edition* and discuss whether or not they find it convincing.	• one copy of *The Case for Faith—Student Edition* per student	10 to 15 minutes

Quick Look ... continued

Activity	Materials needed	Approximate time
3. Time Lines and Demonstration: Does Evolution Explain the Origin of Life? Students will work in teams to research issues of evolution and intelligent design, then create a time line or present a demonstration.	• *The Case for Faith—Student Edition* • paper • markers • masking tape • letter tiles from a Scrabble game (for other options, see the FYI box in activity 3)	25 to 30 minutes
4. Affirmation: Fearfully and Wonderfully Made: Students will write acrostics for one another affirming each person's uniqueness.	• Bible • paper • pens	5 to 10 minutes

1. Object Lesson: The Falling Apple

Tell students that since today's session focuses on science, you would like them to use the scientific method: observation, hypothesis, prediction, and experimentation.

One at a time, hold up several items—a pen, a book, someone's shoe—and drop them. Ask students what they observe about the behavior of the objects. (They fall.)

Ask students to take step 2 of the scientific method: to make a hypothesis about why the objects fall. (The law of gravity.)

Hold up an apple and ask students to predict what will happen if you drop it. Don't drop the apple yet, though. Ask questions like, **According to the law of gravity, this apple ought to fall to the floor, right? It would be impossible for it to stop in mid-air? So if I told you about an apple stopping in mid-air, would you say I must be mistaken?**

Tell students you'll now move to step 4 of the scientific method, experimentation, to see if the prediction is correct. Drop the apple and catch it with your other hand. Continue holding it where you caught it and point out that the apple has done the "impossible"—it has stopped in mid-air. Make the point by saying something like this: **Have I negated the law of gravity? No. I've just intervened. And that's simply what God does when he performs a miracle. He doesn't suspend the laws of nature; he simply chooses to intervene. If I can intervene to catch an apple before it hits the floor, then surely God can intervene in a similar way to accomplish what he wants to accomplish.**

Explain that one of the objections to faith you're going to explore today is the objection that science rules out the possibility of miracles. Ask: **Do you think it's possible to respect science and the laws of nature and still believe in miracles? Explain.** Students should be able to apply the point of the object lesson to respond to this question; if they don't, remind them of what they observed.

FYI

If your students have read Objection #3 in **The Case for Faith—Student Edition,** at some point someone will catch on that you are replicating the example in the box "Miracles and the Laws of Nature" on page 31. If someone says you could catch the apple, don't think of this as spoiling your object lesson. Instead, be glad that your students remember what they read! Incorporate the remark into your lesson by catching the apple and proceeding with the object lesson from that point.

Lee Strobel, the author of *The Case for Faith,* concluded that miracles don't make sense if there is no God—if there is no one to intervene as I did when I caught the apple. But he concluded that miracles can happen if God exists to intervene. What do you think of that logic?

Explain that you'll spend a little time exploring whether or not there are valid reasons to believe that God does in fact exist.

2. Skimming: Top Five Reasons to Give God the Benefit of the Doubt

Make sure everyone has a copy of *The Case for Faith—Student Edition.* Have students turn to page 32. Work through the "Top Five Reasons to Give God the Benefit of the Doubt" by inviting volunteers to read the text and the quotes to consider, then briefly discussing any reactions students have to the material before moving on to the next point.

> **FYI**
>
> Your goal in this activity is simply to get this information to your students quickly and efficiently to lay the groundwork for your discussion of evolution. For most students, the question of evolution is more pertinent than miracles in general, so move through this section quickly to allow enough time for the rest of the session.

Don't read and discuss the box "Random Chance?" on page 34 at this point; save it to discuss in activity 3.

After "Reason #5: God Can Be Immediately Experienced" on page 38, invite students to share times when they experienced God's presence. Be ready with an example of your own. If time permits or if students don't have anything to share, you can read the section "A Knock on the Door" (pp. 38–40) as an example of experiencing God personally. If students offer examples of their own, you don't need to read this section.

3. Time Lines and Demonstration: Does Evolution Explain the Origin of Life?

Form three "research teams." Provide the following materials:

- Team 1: Student sheet 2-1, paper, markers, masking tape
- Team 2: Student sheet 2-2, paper, markers
- Team 3: Student sheet 2-3, letter tiles from a Scrabble game

Give the teams about 10 minutes to do the research and complete the projects described on the student sheets. Then gather the teams back together and have them present their projects.

FYI

If you can't get Scrabble letters, substitute another prop that students can use to create the same effect. Some ideas include

- Dominoes: Throw them randomly and see if they match up; arrange them so that they match (five dots on one domino next to five dots on another, etc.).
- Letter cubes from a Boggle game: The same idea as Scrabble letters on a smaller scale.
- Deck of cards: Shuffle and see if the suits randomly fall into order.

Help students reflect on their own beliefs about science and God by discussing questions like the following:

- **Which of the evidence presented today do you find most convincing? Why?**
- **Would you say there is a convincing case that science does not disprove the existence of God? Explain.**
- **What questions do you still have—either questions you wonder about yourself or you know other people wonder about—regarding science and faith?** (If students raise questions you will address in later sessions, let them know. Otherwise, answer their questions if you can, or point them to the resources listed on page 49 of *The Case for Faith—Student Edition.*)

4. Affirmation: Fearfully and Wonderfully Made

Hand out Bibles and have someone read aloud Psalm 139:13–16. Point out that this passage is a poetic way of talking about the amazing complexity scientists observe in the human body.

Hand out paper and pens and have each student write his or her first name horizontally along the left side of the paper. Collect the papers and say something like this: **In a moment I'm going to hand these papers out randomly. Your job is to write a word or phrase starting with each letter of the name you receive. That word or phrase should be something positive about how that person is "fearfully and wonderfully made." For instance, for Adam you could write,**

- **Awesomely complex**
- **Designed by a master artist**
- **A friendly, funny guy**
- **Makes us laugh**

When you're done, hand your paper back to me so it remains anonymous. Circulate as students write to make sure no one writes anything hurtful or inappropriate. When you have all the papers, read them aloud, then give each person his or her name to take home.

Looking Ahead . . .

If you are assigning reading outside of class, have students read Objection #4 in *The Case for Faith—Student Edition* before the next session.

PRAYER OPTIONS

If your group already has a particular way they like to pray together, work it into the session wherever it fits best. Otherwise, try one of the ideas suggested at the end of session 1.

SESSION 3

Is It Intolerant to Claim Jesus Is the Only Way to God?

(Objection #4 in *The Case for Faith—Student Edition*)

Session goals:

In this session, students will

- identify objections they have heard about Jesus as the only way to God
- explore responses to the objection that Christianity is intolerant
- express their own responses to the issue
- journal to summarize and synthesize what they have learned

Quick Look

Activity	Materials needed	Approximate time
1. Opener: Taste Test: Students will vote for the best soft drink in a taste test, then compare taste preferences with the way people view religion as a matter of personal preference.	• two different kinds of soft drinks, with the labels covered or removed • paper cups • paper • pen	5 to 10 minutes
2. Role Plays: Is Christianity Intolerant? Students will role play objections and responses to Christianity as an intolerant religion.	• Bibles • one copy of *The Case for Faith—Student Edition* per student • student sheet 2-1, cut apart	15 to 20 minutes
3. Discussion: Personal Responses: Students will give personal reactions to questions about why people object to Christianity.	• *The Case for Faith—Student Edition*	5 to 10 minutes

Quick Look . . . continued

Activity	Materials needed	Approximate time
4. Journaling: Putting It All Together: Students will journal as if writing a letter to God or to a friend on the issue of whether or not Christianity is intolerant.	• copies of student sheet 2-2 • pens	5 to 10 minutes

FYI

Your students have grown up with the message that diversity, pluralism, and tolerance are to be embraced. For many, those values have carried over into their view of people's religious convictions. Even the committed Christians in your group may face this objection to Christianity as something that troubles them, not just as an objection they want to be able to refute. Don't come down heavy on it as the wrong attitude; instead, use this session to help students recognize that they don't have to apologize for saying that Jesus is the only way.

1. Opener: Taste Test

Before this session, set out two bottles of soft drinks. Make sure the labels are covered or removed so that kids can't identify them. By each bottle, put a piece of paper.

As students arrive, invite them to participate in a taste test. Let them sample each soft drink, then put a tally mark on the paper by the drink they prefer.

After everyone has tasted, tally the votes and reveal the brands of the soft drinks.

Debrief the experience with questions like these:

- **Would you say we have conclusively determined which soft drink is better?** (It's okay if students disagree.)

- **How do you usually react when someone tells you his or her choice is the "right" choice and yours is the "wrong" choice?**
- **How is this taste test like the way people feel about different religions?**

If students don't bring it up themselves, state that many people feel there is no "right" or "wrong" religion; rather, it's a matter of personal preference. Ask students to share any experiences they have had with this view.

2. Role Plays: Is Christianity Intolerant?

Before you discuss the objection that Christianity is intolerant, make sure students understand Jesus does indeed claim to be the only way to God and his followers affirm he is the only means to salvation. Hand out Bibles and have volunteers read the following verses aloud:

- John 14:6
- Acts 4:12

Next, form three groups. (Each group should be no larger than eight people. If you have more than twenty-four students, form additional groups and have more than one group work on the same role play.) Give each group one of the cut-apart sections of student sheet 3-1. Give instructions like these: **You have 10 minutes to develop a role play. Using the sections of *The Case for Faith—Student Edition* listed on your slip, work as a group to develop a response to the objection on your slip. Then choose one or more people from your group to play the objector, and one or more people to respond. The objector(s) may come back with other comments after the initial response, and so may the responder(s). Be ready to perform your role play for the other groups.**

Let groups work for about 10 minutes, then bring them back together to present their role plays. After each, ask,

- **If you were responding to this objection, is there anything you would add to what has already been said?**
- **If you were the one raising this objection, would you be satisfied with the response? Explain. What other questions or objections might you raise?**

> **FYI**
> The biggest challenge in role plays is knowing when and how to stop. Don't be afraid to cut role plays off if the dialogue is going nowhere.

3. Discussion: Personal Responses

Invite students to listen to the following excerpts and give their own personal responses to the questions asked:

- **When the author, Lee Strobel, asked why more people don't recognize Christianity as the truth, Ravi Zacharias responded, "Because Christ calls you to die to yourself. Whenever truth involves a total commitment, people resist. Christ demands more than most people are willing to give"** (p. 56, *The Case for Faith—Student Edition*). **Do you agree or disagree? Explain.**
- Invite students to take turns reading aloud the boxes on the dateline across the bottom of pages 56 and 57 of *The Case for Faith—Student Edition*. Rephrase the "Today" box as a question for your students: **Do you think abuses in church history are valid reasons to reject Jesus Christ? Why or why not?**
- Read aloud the following excerpt from *The Case for Christ—Student Edition* (pp. 29–30), in which Lee Strobel also deals with the objection that Christianity is intolerant:

  One of Jesus' most outrageous claims is this: "I am the way and the truth and the life. No one comes to the Father except through me" (John 14:6).

Of all the incredible statements Jesus made, this is the one I found most offensive. If anyone else said it, he'd be blasted as exclusive, intolerant, and narrow-minded. It's one thing to claim to be *a* way—but the *only* way to God? That sounds pretty judgmental.

The world is full of religions. The U.S. Constitution even defends your right to believe any religion you choose (or to believe none at all). Legally (at least in the United States), all religions are basically equal. A lot of people will tell you that there are a variety of paths people can take in their spiritual journey, and they all lead to the same God.

But as I looked into the claims of Christianity, I discovered one big difference between it and other religions. Other religions are based on people *doing* something to earn the good favor of God. They must perform good deeds, chant the right words, use a Tibetan prayer wheel, go through a series of reincarnations, or faithfully follow some other religious drills.

By contrast, Christianity is based on what, according to the Bible, Christ has already *done* on the cross. According to the Bible, nobody can do anything to *earn* God's favor— but Jesus offers forgiveness and eternal life as a gift.

Imagine two college frat houses. The first has a strict set of rules and allows in only people who have earned their membership. You have to accomplish something, get top grades, or measure up to a long list of requirements to qualify. No matter how hard they try, a lot of people just won't make the cut. They'll be excluded. That's what every other religion

is like, because they're all based on the system of people doing something to earn God's approval.

But the other house throws its door wide open and says, "Anybody who wants membership is invited inside! Rich or poor, black or white, honor student or rebel, we would love to include you. All you need to get in is to accept this invitation." That, according to the Bible, is what Christianity is like.

Is Christ being offensive when he says that he is the *only* way to God? Judging by the number of people who are offended, you'd better believe it! Is Christ being exclusive? That's a different question. What do you think?

4. Journaling: Putting It All Together

Hand out pens and copies of student sheet 3-2. Read the directions aloud and allow students about 5 minutes to journal independently. When most students are done, invite volunteers to share what they have written.

> **FYI**
>
> If you don't have time to discuss all three excerpts, choose the one or two you think are most relevant to your students.

Looking Ahead . . .

If you are assigning reading outside of class, have students read Objection #5 in *The Case for Faith—Student Edition* before the next session.

> **PRAYER OPTIONS**
>
> If your group already has a particular way they like to pray together, work it into the session wherever it fits best. Otherwise, try one of the ideas suggested at the end of session 1.

SESSION 4

How Could a Loving God Send People to Hell?

(Objection #5 in *The Case for Faith—Student Edition*)

Session goals:

In this session, students will

- brainstorm what they know or have heard about hell
- discuss questions and answers about hell
- receive assurance that hell cannot overpower those who believe in Christ
- hear the challenge to share the gospel with those who do not believe

Quick Look

Activity	Materials needed	Approximate time
1. Brainstorming: What Do You Know?: Students will list everything they know or have heard about hell, then discuss whether the statements are true or false.	• newsprint or whiteboard or chalkboard • marker or chalk	10 to 15 minutes
2. Discussion: Q&A: Students will discuss the questions and answers in Objection #5 of *The Case for Faith—Student Edition.*	• a copy of *The Case for Faith – Student Edition* for each student • Bibles	30 to 35 minutes
3. Challenge: The Gates of Hell: Students will study Matthew 16:16–19 for encouragement and motivation to reach out to others.	• Bibles	5 to 10 minutes

1. Brainstorming: What Do You Know?

Ask students to tell you everything they know about hell or have heard about hell—whether it's right or wrong. Write all their responses on newsprint, a whiteboard, or a chalkboard.

When all their ideas are in writing, go over the list one statement at a time, asking, **Is this true?** If students think a statement is false, cross it out. If they're not sure, put a question mark by it.

2. Discussion: Q&A

Have students turn to Objection #5 on page 63 in *The Case for Faith—Student Edition.* Ask them to flip through the chapter looking for any questions that address any of the statements on the brainstormed list. As they find relevant questions, have a volunteer read the answer aloud. Have Bibles handy so you can look up and read any Scripture references.

If the question in the book deals with a statement the students decided was either true or false, discuss whether the answer in the book confirms or disputes the students' opinion. If the question in the book deals with a statement students were undecided on, ask students whether the answer in the book helps them decide whether the statement on their brainstormed list is true or false.

When students have read and discussed all the Q&As relating to their brainstormed list, have them choose other questions in the chapter they would like to discuss.

3. Challenge: The Gates of Hell

Hand out Bibles and have students follow along as a volunteer reads Matthew 16:16–19 aloud. Ask:

- **What do you think it means that the gates of Hades, or hell, will not overcome the church (v. 18)?**
- **What comfort can that give you if you are one who believes that Jesus is the Son of God (v. 16)?**
- **What do you think verse 19 means?** Supplement students' responses with this note from *The Quest Study Bible* (Zondervan, 1994): "Jesus gave Peter and the other apostles spiritual authority to preach the gospel and thus open the door of his kingdom both to Jews and Gentiles (Acts 2:14–41; 10:22–48)."
- **How will you respond to this passage? Do you need to accept Jesus as the Son of God? Or, if you've done that already, do you need to express your thanks to God that hell has no power over you? Is there someone you need to talk to about Jesus so the door of the kingdom will be open to that person and they won't have to face hell?**

Invite students to spend a few minutes in silent prayer or reflection.

FYI

Verse 20 isn't part of your study, but perhaps a student will read ahead and ask how preaching the gospel (see note on verse 19) fits with not telling anyone that Jesus is the Christ. Use this note from *The Quest Study Bible* (Zondervan, 1994) to help clarify: "Before they could tell the news accurately, the disciples first needed to learn more about what it *meant* to say that Jesus was the Christ. Faulty ideas about the Messiah were common among the people who expected an earthly or militaristic kingdom. It's obvious the disciples did not understand Jesus well enough yet, for at this time even Peter (who stated his belief in v. 16) found it difficult to accept Jesus' coming suffering (v. 22.)"

Looking Ahead ...

If you are assigning reading outside of class, have students read Objection #6 in *The Case for Faith—Student Edition* before the next session.

PRAYER OPTIONS

If your group already has a particular way they like to pray together, work it into the session wherever it fits best. Otherwise, try one of the ideas suggested at the end of session 1.

SESSION 5

If I Have Doubts, Can I Be a Christian?

(Objection #6 in *The Case for Faith—Student Edition*)

Session goals:

In this session, students will

- express how doubt impacts their own lives
- explore misconceptions about faith and doubt
- identify specific ways to strengthen their faith

Quick Look

Activity	Materials needed	Approximate time
1. Acting: Faith and Doubt in the Bible: Students will act out Mark 9:14-27, then discuss whether or not faith and doubt can coexist.	• Bible	10 to 15 minutes
2. Self-test: Doubters' Anonymous: Students will assess how doubt impacts their lives.	• copies of student sheet 5-1 • pens • one copy of *The Case for Faith—Student Edition* for each student	10 to 15 minutes
3. Bible Study: What Faith Isn't: Students will read Psalm 22 and discuss the relationship between faith, feelings, and doubt.	• Bibles • completed student sheets from activity 2	10 to 15 minutes
4. Goal-Setting: Dealing with Doubt: Students will identify specific ways to strengthen their faith.	• *The Case for Faith—Student Edition* • pens	10 to 15 minutes

1. Acting: Faith and Doubt in the Bible

Assign students the following roles:

- Jesus
- father (identified in verse 16 as "a man in the crowd"
- boy
- disciples (1 or more students)
- crowd (optional: as few or as many as you wish)

Read Mark 9:14–27 aloud and have students act out their roles as you read.

Ask:

- **Would you say the father in this event had faith or doubts? Explain.**
- **What do you think he meant by "I do believe; help me overcome my unbelief?"**
- **Do you think it's possible to have belief and unbelief, faith and doubts, at the same time? Explain.**

2. Self-test: Doubters' Anonymous

Have students form groups of three. Hand out pens and copies of student sheet 5-1, and allow students a few minutes to complete their sheets. Then have them share what they marked with the other members of their threesome.

3. Bible Study: What Faith Isn't

When most groups are done, gather them back into one group. Ask:

- **What do you think the relationship is between faith and feelings?**
- **What do you think it should be?**

> **FYI**
>
> By now your students should have enough sense of community that they will be willing to share on this level in a small group. Don't worry about those students who aren't willing to share; they may not give completely open responses, but they will still think about their own level of doubt.

Hand out Bibles and have students follow along while a volunteer reads Psalm 22:1–8. Ask:

- **How would you say the writer of this psalm is doing emotionally?**
- **Do you recognize these words from any other event?** (If students don't identify them as Christ's words from the cross, have someone read Matthew 27:45–46.)
- **What kinds of emotions do you think Jesus was experiencing?**
- **Do you think Jesus' faith was weak because his emotions were so troubled and he was in such a painful situation? Explain.**

Have someone read Psalm 22:9, 22–23 aloud. Ask:

- **Judging from these verses, would you say that the writer's faith went up and down with his emotions? Explain.**
- ***The Case for Faith—Student Edition* says, "It's normal to mix up faith and emotions. Sometimes that can leave us longing for a spiritual high—and wondering who's at fault, us or God, if we don't feel it. . . . We need to learn that faith is not always about having positive feelings toward God or life" (pp. 77–78, 79). Based on what you've observed about this psalm-writer and about Jesus, would you agree or disagree with that statement? Explain.**

Ask students to share their responses to the last two statements on the student sheet and discuss their responses. Remind them of the father in the biblical episode they acted out at the beginning of the session to assure them they can believe and still struggle with doubt.

4. Goal-Setting: Dealing with Doubt

Summarize the material in the section "Dealing with Doubt" (pp. 81–84) in *The Case for Faith—Student Edition* as follows:

- **The first step in dealing with doubt is to choose to believe. Commit to following God and don't quit.**

FYI

Different theological traditions have varying views about whether an individual chooses to believe or whether God chooses that individual to believe. Either way, Scripture is clear that believers are called to put their hand to the plow and not look back (Luke 9:62). Phrase the first step in whatever way is consistent with your theological position.

- **The second step is to go where faith is.** Have someone read aloud the section "Go Where Faith Is" on pages 82–83 of *The Case for Faith—Student Edition.* Then point students to the "Personal Planner" box on page 83 and have them spend a few minutes filling it in for themselves. Invite students to share what "works" for them. This can be the most helpful part of the session as mature believers motivate other students to pursue missions trips, personal devotions, or whatever has been meaningful to them in their faith development.
- **The last—but not least—step is to put your faith in the right place. As Lynn Anderson says in *The Case for Faith—Student Edition,* you can have a lot of faith in thin ice, but it will still let you down.**

Take this opportunity to share your own testimony of Jesus as the only one worth investing faith in. Invite students to make a commitment to Christ if they haven't done so.

Close your time together by praying for God to work in the lives of your students, creating faith where there is none, strengthening faith where there is doubt.

Why Does God Allow Suffering?

If there is a God, why didn't he make a world where people don't hurt each other? Read Genesis 1:1, 10, 25, 31 and Genesis 3:1–19. Based on those passages, how would you respond to this question? Jot your answer here.

Investigation 1: Is Suffering God's Fault?

Now read the section "Is It God's Fault?" on pages 13–17 of *The Case for Faith—Student Edition.* How does that section add to your understanding of this issue? As a small group, come up with a response to the question, "Is suffering God's fault?" and jot it here. Be ready to share it and explain it.

Why Does God Allow Suffering?

If God is all-powerful and all-loving, why doesn't he just wipe out all suffering? Read Romans 5:3. Based on that passage, how would you respond to this question? Jot your answer here.

Investigation 2: Suffering as Training?

Now read the section "Training" on page 19 of *The Case for Faith—Student Edition.* How does that section add to your understanding of this issue? Jot your response here. Be ready to share it and explain it.

Why Does God Allow Suffering?

If God is all-powerful and all-loving, why doesn't he just wipe out all suffering? Read Hebrews 12:10–11. Based on that passage, how would you respond to this question? Jot your answer here.

Investigation 3: Suffering as a Midcourse Correction?

Now read the section "Midcourse Correction" on pages 20 and 21 of *The Case for Faith—Student Edition.* How does that section add to your understanding of this issue? Jot your response here. Be ready to share it and explain it.

Why Does God Allow Suffering?

If God is all-powerful and all-loving, why doesn't he just wipe out all suffering? Read Romans 8:28. Based on that passage, how would you respond to this question? Jot your answer here.

Investigation 4: Positive from Negative

Now read the section "Positive from Negative" on pages 21 and 22 of *The Case for Faith—Student Edition.* How does that section add to your understanding of this issue? Jot your response here. Be ready to share it and explain it.

Why Does God Allow Suffering?

If God is all-powerful and all-loving, why doesn't he just wipe out all suffering? Read Psalm 18:4–6. According to that passage, what might suffering lead a person to do? How might that be a positive outcome? Jot your answer here.

Investigation 5: Getting Your Attention

Now read the section "Getting Your Attention" on page 19 and the box "The Megaphone of Pain" on page 24 of *The Case for Faith—Student Edition.* How do those sections add to your understanding of this issue? Jot your response here. Be ready to share it and explain it.

Why Does God Allow Suffering?

How can a just and loving God allow people to get away with causing others to suffer? Isn't that unfair? Read Revelation 21:3–4 and 2 Peter 3:9. Based on those passages, how would you respond to this question? Jot your answer here.

Investigation 6: Is God Unfair?

Now read the section "It Isn't Fair" on pages 24–25 of *The Case for Faith—Student Edition.* (You can skip the box "The Megaphone of Pain," but read "Taking the Long View.") How does that section add to your understanding of this issue? Jot your response here. Be ready to share it and explain it.

Research Team 1: Micro- vs. Macro-Evolution

Your project is to research theories of micro- and macro-evolution and how they relate to theories about the development of different species. You will find the information you need in the section "Micro- vs. Macro-Evolution" on pages 42–44 of *The Case for Faith—Student Edition.*

You will develop a time line to show various scientific findings and theories over the years. For each date on your time line, use one sheet of paper that clearly shows the date. Write and provide illustrations for the relevant information for that date on the paper. Your time line must include the following:

- 1859: Darwin's theory of the origin of species. Summarize Darwin's theory. Include and define the terms "micro-evolution" and "macro-evolution."
- 1979: Fossil evidence regarding species.
- Today: Summarize your conclusions, responses, and/or questions about this issue. If you agree as a team, you can write one summary. If different opinions are represented on your team, summarize each one.

When you have completed the dates for your time line, work with Research Team 2 to post them chronologically on the wall. Research Team 2 will have other dates to include on the time line.

If you finish before the other teams, you may add other dates to your time line. They don't have to be related to evolution!

Research Team 2: How Life Began

Your project is to research theories of how life began. You will find the information you need in the sections "Origin of Life," "Miller-Urey Experiment," and "More Recent Theories" on pages 44–46 of *The Case for Faith—Student Edition.*

You will develop a time line to show various scientific findings and theories over the years. For each date on your time line, use one sheet of paper that clearly shows the date. Write and provide illustrations for the relevant information for that date on the paper. Your time line must include the following:

- 1668: Francesco Redi's discovery and its impact on theories of life.
- 1859: Darwin's theory of the origin of life.
- 1953: Miller-Urey experiment.
- 1980: NASA conclusions.
- Today: Summarize your conclusions, responses, and/or questions about this issue. If you agree as a team, you can write one summary. If different opinions are represented on your team, summarize each one.

When you have completed the dates for your time line, work with Research Team 1 to post them chronologically on the wall. Research Team 1 will have other dates to include on the time line.

If you finish before the other teams, you may add other dates to your time line. They don't have to be related to evolution!

Research Team 3: Random Chance or Intelligent Design?

Your project is to research theories of random chance and intelligent design as origins of life. You will find the information you need on the random chance theory on page 41 of *The Case for Faith—Student Edition.* You will find information on the theory of intelligent design in the sections "Random Chance?" and "An Intelligent Designer?" on pages 46–48 of *The Case for Faith—Student Edition.* Also read the box "Random Chance?" on page 34.

You will develop a demonstration to show how each theory suggests life came into existence. Use the Scrabble letters or other supplies provided as the building blocks of "life." If you're stuck for ideas on how to do this, read again the analogy of DNA as written language in the section "Intelligent Designer" on pages 47–48 of *The Case for Faith—Student Edition.*

Be prepared to present your demonstration to the other research teams, along with your conclusions. If team members do not all draw the same conclusions, present the differing opinions.

Role Play Slips

Photocopy and cut apart this page. Hand out the cut-apart sections as directed in activity 2 of session 3.

Objection:	Response:
I'm not necessarily against religion, but I could never accept Christianity. It's such an intolerant religion! If I did choose a religion, I'd choose one that's more tolerant, like maybe Buddhism or Hinduism.	[Read the section "Alone in Intolerance?" on page 52 of *The Case for Faith—Student Edition,* and come up with a good response to this objection. Be ready to give your response in a role play.]

Objection:	Response:
When you get right down to it, all the world religions are pretty much the same. So they're all equally right.	[Read the section "Remember the Elephant" up through the chart "God or No God?" on pages 52-53 of *The Case for Faith—Student Edition,* and come up with a good response to this objection. Be ready to give your response in a role play.]

Objection:	Response:
Christianity may be true for you, but that doesn't mean Buddhism isn't true for someone else. It's intolerant to claim that only one religion is true.	[Read the section "Remember the Elephant" starting after the chart "God or No God?" on page 53 of *The Case for Faith—Student Edition*, the section "Many Truths," and the box "Schizophrenic God," and come up with a good response to this objection. Be ready to give your response in a role play.]

Putting It All Together

Take a few minutes to reflect on what you've been exploring during this session. Then write a letter. You won't have to send it, and you won't have to share it unless you want to.

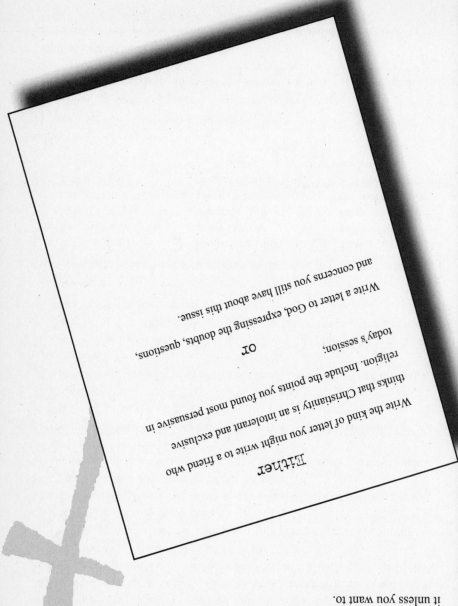

Either

Write the kind of letter you might write to a friend who thinks that Christianity is an intolerant and exclusive religion. Include the points you found most persuasive in today's session;

or

Write a letter to God, expressing the doubts, questions, and concerns you still have about this issue.

Doubters' Anonymous

Check the box that best describes you.

- ☐ The church kid: You've grown up in church and you consider yourself a Christian—but sometimes you find yourself wondering if it's really all true.
- ☐ The smoke screen: Your doubts aren't so much about whether or not God is real. They're more about whether or not you can really change your lifestyle to live the way you know God asks you to.
- ☐ The disappointed: God hasn't answered your prayers or met your needs. So you wonder, "*Is God really there?*"
- ☐ The wounded: Abuse or rejection or some kind of suffering makes you ask, "*If there's a God, why does he let this happen?*"
- ☐ The rebel: You don't want to follow your parents' lead, so you rebel against the God they believe in.
- ☐ The independent: You're not going to let anybody—not even God—run your life.
- ☐ The uncommitted: You want to keep your options open. There are a lot of points of view and a lot of lifestyles out there. Commitment to Christ isn't for you right now.
- ☐ The worshiper with the blahs: You go to church, but you don't seem to get as much out of it as other people do. You've started to wonder, "*Is there something wrong with me—or something wrong with God?*"

When it comes to the relationship between my faith and my emotions, usually . . .

- ☐ if I'm feeling low, my faith is low; if I'm feeling good, my faith is strong
- ☐ how strong I feel in my faith is somewhat influenced by my emotions at the time
- ☐ I know that God is real and that he loves me even if I don't necessarily feel his presence or his love

I think

- ☐ having a strong faith means never having doubts.
- ☐ it's possible to have doubts even when you believe.
- ☐ facing doubts can help you develop a stronger faith than if you never doubt.

I think the opposite of faith is

- ☐ doubt—serious questions about what I believe or about whether or not God is real and the Bible is true.
- ☐ unbelief—a willful refusal to believe or a deliberate decision to disobey God.

Two Short Scripts

The Case for Faith—Student Edition

How to use these scripts. These scripts allow your students to present two short sketches depicting "before" and "after" scenes. Script 1, the "before" scene, highlights the need for convincing evidence for the case for faith. Script 2, "after," shows how being equipped with evidence can give believers confidence in sharing their faith and give seekers the evidence they need to make a decision in faith.

Consider these options for using the sketches:

- Present Script 1 to your youth group to promote the study of *The Case for Faith—Student Edition.* Use Script 2 to celebrate what they've learned at the end of the course.
- Present the sketches to the whole church to highlight what the youth group is doing. You can present Script 1 at the beginning of your course, then Script 2 at the conclusion, or you can present them back-to-back at the end of the course.
- Use the sketches to promote a study for adults of *The Case for Faith.*

Staging the sketches. Use your students as actors. There's a part for you, too! Photocopy the scripts so every player has one. Nonspeaking parts are flexible in number so that you can involve all your students. Keep sets and props simple; let the audience rely on their imaginations. Tips for sets and staging are included in the scripts.

You can adapt the sketches to your own setting by using your students' real names, replacing the activities mentioned with things your students do together, and so on. Have fun!

Script 1: Before

Cast:

3 Christian students: Christians 1, 2, & 3 (use the students' real names)

Hurting friend

Teacher

Classmates (as few or as many students as you have; assign the "classmates" lines any way you wish)

2 "tolerant" friends

Youth leader

[NOTE: If you don't have enough students to fill all these parts, you can use one Christian student. Double up other roles as needed.]

Setting: Designate three separate areas of your stage or performance space as follows:

Scene 1: 2 chairs, back-to-back; 2 phones

Scene 2: chairs set in rows facing the audience to represent a schoolroom; if you have the space and props, add a teacher's desk and globe, a chalkboard, etc.

Scene 3: a small table, 3 chairs, and paper cups from McDonald's, Starbucks, or wherever your students like to hang out.

Have all the actors get into their places before the sketch begins. To focus attention on only one setting at a time, have the actors in the other settings freeze when it is not their scene. If you can use lighting to spotlight each setting in its scene, go for it.

Scene 1:

Youth leader: [center stage] Have you ever heard people tell you what a wonderful, carefree time of life youth is? I don't think those people realize the challenges to faith that students face today.

[moving to set 1] Take Christian 1 [use real name], for example. She's just received the bad news that her friend's brother was hit by a drunk driver. The doctors had to amputate his leg; they're still not sure he'll survive. Let's listen in as ______________ [Christian 1] calls her friend.

Christian 1: [sitting in chair, talking on phone] Kendra, I'm so sorry! I just heard about your brother. How are you doing?

Kendra: [in other chair, on other phone] I . . . I don't know. It doesn't seem real. But when I saw him in the hospital, all bandaged up and unconscious—that was real. Oh, ________, it's just so awful!

Christian 1: Is there anything I can do? You know I'm here for you.

Kendra: I don't know. I don't think there's anything anyone can do.

Christian 1: Well, let me know. And, Kendra . . .

Kendra: Yeah?

Christian 1: I'll be praying for your brother.

Kendra: Praying?! Don't bother! God doesn't care what happens to my brother! If he did, this would never have happened.

Christian 1: Oh, Kendra! That's not true!

Kendra: Oh, no? Where was God when that drunk driver got behind the wheel and cost my brother his leg!

Christian 1: Well . . . uh . . . I guess I'm not sure, but I know God cares.

Kendra: I'm sorry, _____________, but I just can't believe that a caring God would let something like this happen.

[Christian 1 and Kendra freeze.]

Youth leader: What would *you* say to Kendra? [to audience]

Scene 2

Youth leader: [moving to set 2] Now let's look in on Christian 2 [again, use a real name]. His biology teacher has just finished explaining how the theory of evolution provides a scientific understanding of the origin of life.

Teacher: Any questions, class? [Christian 2 hesitantly raises his hand.] Yes, ______________ [name].

Christian 2: Um, I'm afraid this might be a stupid question.

Teacher: No, ______________, there are no stupid questions.

Christian 2: Well, I don't quite get how God fits in.

Classmate: That *is* a stupid question!

Teacher: [to Classmate] Excuse me?

Classmate: Well, if evolution explains the origin of life, then God doesn't fit in.

Classmate 2: Yeah. The idea of some miraculous creation or something—I mean, science proves that miracles can't happen.

Classmate: Just look at the evidence, ______________ [Christian 2]. Science or religion—intelligent thought or wishful thinking. You can't have them both.

Teacher: Well, __________________ [Christian 2]?

Christian 2: Uh . . .

[All freeze.]

Youth leader: [to audience] If you were in ____________'s [Christian 2's] class, would you have the evidence you need to show that the Christian faith is more than wishful thinking?

Scene 3

Youth leader: [moving to set 3] Here's ____________ [Christian 3,] hanging out with some friends at Starbucks [choose a hot spot for your students]. Let's listen in.

Friend 1: I am so stressed out! I mean, with school, and my parents always on my case, and never knowing whether Tyler is going to call or not—I'm about to spazz out!

Christian 3: Tell me about it! It's like this is the only time all week I've even had time to talk to you guys! I'm sooo busy!

Friend 2: Ooh, you guys—you gotta try this new thing I just learned. It's like life therapy, or something, and it's so awesome for centering yourself.

Friend 1: Life therapy? Like counseling?

Friend 2: No—it's all holistic and spiritual. You get these candles and focus on your inner self, then you . . . well, I can show you better than I can explain it. Want to come to my house and try it?

Friend 1: Sure. It can't hurt.

Christian 3: I don't know. What do you mean when you say it's spiritual?

Friend 2: Oh, you know, kind of Zen and stuff.

Christian 3: You know I'm a Christian. I'm not into that stuff.

Friend 2: Oh, don't be so narrow-minded.

Friend 3: Really. I mean, it's not like your way is the only way.

Friend 2: I mean, Christianity might be true for you. I can respect that. But this is true for me.

Friend 3: I don't think you have to worry about it, ____________ [Christian 3]. After all, all religions ultimately point to the same God, don't they?

Christian 3: I don't think so . . .

Friend 2: Oh, don't be so intolerant!

[All freeze.]

Scene 4

Youth leader: [moving to center stage]: Have you ever found yourself in a situation like one of these? If you have, you know that it can make you doubt your ability to make a case for faith—maybe even make you doubt your faith itself.

[Christians 1, 2, and 3 approach Youth leader.]

Christian 1: Hey, _______________ [Youth leader], can I talk to you?

Youth leader: Sure. What's up?

Christian 1: Well, it's my friend Kendra. She's going through a pretty hard time, and . . . well, I was wondering if God is really there for her like I always thought he was.

Youth leader: Do you know what God promises in the Bible?

Christian 1: Yeah. It's just . . . I'm not so sure it's always true anymore.

Christian 2: I know what you mean. I've been to Sunday school and church and all that, and I always thought I believed it all—but sometimes I wonder whether I believed it just because that's what was expected of me. Maybe I'm a Christian because my parents are, not because it's really true.

Christian 3: Exactly! I know some people get all these thrills and chills when they worship Jesus, but really I don't feel all that excited most of the time. I'd like to be pumped up about God, but I just don't know . . . He doesn't always seem real to me.

Christian 2: Man, if we have all these doubts, maybe we're not really Christians after all.

Youth leader: Trust me on this one, guys: Asking hard questions doesn't mean the end of your faith. If you really go after the answers, it can be the beginning of a faith that's stronger and more satisfying than you ever imagined!

[Youth leader wraps up with an explanation of what the youth will be studying, or a challenge to adults, or whatever you've decided your purpose is for this sketch.]

Script 2: After

Cast and Setting: the same as for Script 1

Scene 1

Youth leader: [to audience] Remember ____________ [Christian 1] and her doubts about how to respond to her hurting friend? Let's see how she's doing.

Christian 1: Hey, Kendra, it's me again. Just calling to see how you're doing.

Kendra: Oh, hi. I'm okay, I guess. Nothing much has changed.

Christian 1: Listen, Kendra, remember when you asked me how God could let this accident happen to your brother? Well, I've been thinking a lot about that, and I'd be glad to talk with you about it sometime if you want.

Kendra: I don't know. I'm not sure I feel like talking about God right now.

Christian 1: How about if I come over and we just spend some time together? We don't need to talk about anything you don't want to right now—I just wanted to let you know that I'm ready to talk about it whenever you are.

Kendra: Well, I could use some company. Why don't you come over.

Christian 1: I'll be right there.

[Kendra and Christian 1 hang up phones and exit.]

Youth leader: [to audience] Kendra may not be ready to hear what ________________ [Christian 1] has learned about how a good God can allow suffering, but when she is ready, ________________ [Christian 1] will be, too. And in the meantime, she'll be there for Kendra, just as God is here for us.

Scene 2

Youth leader: What about ________________ [Christian 2], the student who found himself without any evidence to back up his belief in a God who created and controls this world? Let's see how he's doing at the end of biology class today.

[Students are picking up books and standing up as if to leave class.]

Classmate: So, ________________ [Christian 2], I bet you're glad we're done studying evolution, huh? The teacher really debunked the idea of creation.

Christian 2: Actually, I've been finding out some things that make me even more convinced that there must be a God who created the world.

Classmate: What—some more religious mumbo-jumbo?

Christian 2: No—scientific discoveries more recent than Darwin's theories, for one thing. And a lot about how incredibly complex the world is. Did you know that lots of scientists—not just Christian ones—think the world is way too complex to have come about by chance? . . .

[Students leave.]

Scene 3

Youth leader: ________________ [Christian 3] is at Starbuck's again with her friends—the ones who don't want to be associated with a religion as "exclusive" and "intolerant" as Christianity. Let's listen in.

Christian 3: So, how's the Zen thing working for you?

Friend 1: Oh, it's awesome! I mean, I'm still stressed out a lot, but that's life, you know?

Friend 2: How about you, ______________, [Christian 3]? Ready to give centering and meditation a try?

Chrisian 3: You know, I don't need to. I've found out that Jesus can help me deal with stress and really live a fulfilling life.

Friend 1: Hey, whatever works for you. Jesus was an awesome teacher.

Christian 3: Yeah, but Jesus is more than that. He's not just *one* way to God and a full life—he's the *only* way.

Friend 2: That's just your opinion, though. My truth is different.

Christian 3: I disagree. I think some things are true, period.

Friend 1: What do you mean?

Christian 3: Well . . . [looking around, then picking up cup so she covers part of it with her hand] . . . Take this cup, for example. How many ounces do you think it holds?

Friend 1: I don't know. Twelve, maybe?

Friend 2: Or sixteen?

Christian 3: But I happen to know it holds fourteen ounces. [moving hand to uncover part of cup] See—it says so right here.

Friend 1: So?

Christian 3: So, that's true, right? Not just true for me, but true for everybody.

Friend 2: Okay. Not that it matters how many ounces a cup holds.

Christian 3: But it does matter what's true about God, doesn't it? Especially when it can make a difference in your whole life?

Friend 1: Well, I guess I see what you're saying. But how can you know what's true?

Christian 3: I was hoping you'd ask!

[All exit.]